D0771394

HONEY

HONEY

A Book of Recipes

INTRODUCTION BY JENNY FLEETWOOD

LORENZ BOOKS
NEW YORK • LONDON • SYDNEY • BATH

Lorenz Books is an imprint of
Anness Publishing Limited
27 West 20th Street
New York, New York 10011

LORENZ BOOKS are available for bulk purchase for sales promotion and
for premium use. For details write or call the manager of special sales:
Lorenz Books, 27 West 20th Street, New York, New York 10011: (212) 807-6739.

ISBN 1 85967 362 7

Publisher: Joanna Lorenz
Senior Cookbook Editor: Linda Fraser
Project Editor: Anne Hildyard
Designer: Bill Mason
Illustrations: Anna Koska

Photographers: Steve Baxter, James Duncan, Michell Garrett,
Nelson Hargreaves, Amanda Heywood, David Jordan, Don Last,
Patrick McLeavey and Thomas Odulate
Recipes: Alex Barker, Kit Chan, Carole Clements, Elizabeth Wolf-Cohen,
Christine France, Sarah Gates, Sue Maggs, Liz Trigg and Pamela Westland
Food for photography: Carla Capalbo, Elizabeth Wolf-Cohen, Carole Handslip,
Wendy Lee, Jane Stevenson and Judy Williams
Stylists: Madeleine Brehaut, Blake Minton, Kirsty Rawlings and Fiona Tillett

Printed in China

1 3 5 7 9 10 8 6 4 2

Contents

$\mathscr{I}$NTRODUCTION

Man's love affair with honey goes back thousands of years. Ancient rock paintings in southern Africa and Spain portray men harvesting wild honey, first by climbing up trees or rock faces, and later using primitive ladders and smoking torches.

The earliest hives were probably accidental – the result of bees nesting in hollow trees, logs or pots – but honey hunters soon discovered that by trapping the queen in a container of their own making, woven perhaps from grass or reeds, they could have easy access to the delicious sweet treat.

The ancient Egyptians were proficient beekeepers, even moving their hives down the Nile, by donkey or boat, as the flowers that furnished the nectar came into bloom. They fed honey cakes to their sacred animals and used honey in many of their rituals, including the ceremonial burial of a pharaoh.

Honey has been used in healing and folk medicine for generations, continues to be featured in face masks and other beauty products and is used to make soothing balms, but it is as a natural sweetener that it is most highly regarded. When the Aztecs found their chocolate a little too bitter, they simply stirred in a little honey. The ancient Greeks and Romans used it to make bread and

cakes, and the French found honey the perfect sweetener for their famous *pain d'épices*. In Germany it surfaced in *lebkuchen*, while the Italians mixed it with nuts, cocoa, spices, candied peel and melon to make the popular *panforte*. Today, honey is just as popular as an ingredient in savory dishes, including salad dressings, casseroles, marinades and glazes for poultry and meat that is to be barbecued.

In Britain, beekeeping is an ancient tradition. The Druids called this land The Isle of Honey, and mead was for centuries the national drink. Mead is still made today, and can be sweet or dry. Honey beer is a favorite in some parts of Africa. Unlike mead, it is made relatively rapidly and is ready to drink 1–2 days after fermentation has begun. The original amber nectar also finds its way into a number of liqueurs, including Drambuie, which is made from Scotch whiskey, herbs and honey scented with heather, and *Krupnik*, which is a Polish whiskey and honey liqueur.

Whatever your favorite drink might be, raise a glass to honey and good health as you leaf through the pages of this book, planning another excellent meal based upon this exciting ingredient.

Jenny Fleetwood

Types of Honey

Orange Blossom
From the orange groves of Spain, Mexico, the USA, Israel and South Africa, this is a clear golden honey with a delicate citrus flavor. It is very good for cooking.

Acacia
This is a very light and delicate honey, ideal for sweetening hot or cold drinks. It tends to stay liquid in the jar, which makes it easy to mix into food or drinks.

Heather
With its subtle woody flavor, heather honey is extremely popular. Creamy in the jar, it liquefies when stirred, so it is convenient to use.

Eucalyptus
Australia is the main source of this creamy honey. There are numerous native species of eucalyptus, so the appearance of the honey varies considerably, but the most commonly exported variety looks a lot like peanut butter and has a distinctive toffeelike flavor.

English Set
Gathered from bees in England, set honey is honey which has been allowed to crystallize naturally.

Clover
North America's most popular honey, this is pale cream in color. It has a smooth, mild flavor. Usually sold as a set honey, it is also available clear.

Honeycomb
This is a delicious treat, sold in health food shops and other specialty food stores. It is very fragile, and is therefore often sold in a miniature wooden frame. The entire comb is edible and is usually served in small squares.

Manuka
This monofloral honey (from a single source) comes from New Zealand. Dark and creamy, it is often packed in a dark amber pot to preserve the color and aroma.

Cut Comb
This is also available at health food stores and specialty shops. As the name suggests, this consists of bars sliced from a large honeycomb and wrapped separately.

Creamed floral and heather

English set

Cut comb honey

Acacia

Canadian clover

New Zealand manuka

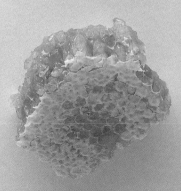

Orange Blossom

Australian eucalyptus

Honeycomb

Basic Techniques

HONEY AND HEALTH

Ever since Athenaeus, a Greek writer and philosopher, asserted in the second century that those who ate honey every day for breakfast would be free from disease for the rest of their lives, extravagant claims have been made about honey. Although there is scant scientific evidence for most of these endorsements – honey is basically sugar – the belief in its medicinal qualities has persisted and is fundamental to folklore the world over.

• Honey is an easily assimilated source of unrefined sugars, and is a useful energy food for athletes.

• Honey is mildly antiseptic. It is used in some Eastern European countries for treating burns and wounds. Some germs cannot survive in honey.

• It is believed that honey is a natural sedative, and can be helpful in reducing stress levels.

• An English book on the properties of honey, published in the 18th century, recommended it for the treatment of asthma, coughs and hoarseness.

Cook's Tips

• For a simply delicious dessert, mix plain yogurt with flaked almonds, then use a honey spoon to drizzle honey over the top.

• Honey is very good in salad dressings. Mix 1 tablespoon clear honey with ⅔ cup white wine vinegar in a screw-top jar. Add plenty of salt and ground black pepper. Close the jar and shake well before using.

• To substitute honey for sugar in baking, use ¾ cup honey for every 1 cup sugar specified. Use slightly less liquid and cook the cake or bread at a slightly lower temperature than the one suggested in the recipe.

• If you need to heat honey, do it very gently. High temperatures destroy the enzymes, may cause the sugar in the honey to caramelize and will almost certainly affect the flavor.

STORING AND USING HONEY

There is no difference, either nutritionally or chemically, between clear (liquid) honey and set honey. Most honey is syrupy when collected. Some types stay that way, but the majority soon start to granulate. What happens is that part of the glucose separates out as crystals. A network is rapidly established, so the honey looks solid. The crystals are pure white, so the honey gets lighter. The person marketing the

honey decides whether it should be clear or set, bearing in mind the honey's natural properties and what the market requires. Americans tend to like their honey clear, but Canadians prefer the set type. Clear honey is heat-treated to discourage granulation; set honey is encouraged to form small evenly distributed crystals, so the honey is smooth, not grainy.

If clear honey granulates, simply place the jar in warm water. Use the same method to liquefy set honey.

It is not necessary – or even desirable – to store honey in the fridge. Keep it in a cool, dry place and it will last for a long time without loss of flavor.

HONEY AND HAZELNUT SPREAD

Try this superb spread on scones or hot toast.

Roast ¾ cup hazelnuts, rub off the skins and grind the nuts in a food processor. Transfer to a bowl and add 3 tablespoons set honey and 2 tablespoons heavy cream. Stir well until mixed, then chill until the spread is set. Use the spread in 1–2 days. Makes about 1 cup.

Savory Snacks
and Side Dishes

Begin your next barbecue with succulent
spare ribs or chicken wings with a honey glaze,
or let your guests guess the identity of the
mystery ingredient that makes the
salmon stir-fry taste so good.

HONEY-GLAZED SPARE RIBS

These delicious sticky ribs are easy to eat with fingers, once the little bones have been cleaned away from one end to provide a handle.

Makes about 25

2½ pounds meaty pork spare ribs,
    cut into 2-inch lengths

¾ cup ketchup or mild
    chili sauce

2–3 tablespoons soy sauce

2–3 tablespoons clear honey

2 garlic cloves, finely chopped

¼ cup orange juice

¼ teaspoon cayenne pepper (or
    to taste)

¼ teaspoon Chinese five-
    spice powder

1–2 whole star anise

COOK'S TIP

Five-spice powder, made from ground cinnamon, star anise, cloves, ginger and fennel seeds, adds a delicious flavor to marinades, cookies and pies.

Using a small sharp knife, scrape away about ¼ inch of meat from one end of each tiny spare rib, to serve as a little handle.

Mix the ketchup, soy sauce, honey, garlic, orange juice, cayenne, five-spice powder and star anise in a large bowl or shallow baking dish until well blended. Add the ribs and toss to coat. Cover and chill for 6–8 hours or overnight.

Preheat the oven to 350°F. Line a baking sheet with foil and arrange the spare ribs in a single layer, spooning over any remaining marinade.

Bake uncovered, basting occasionally, for 1–1½ hours or until the ribs are well browned and glazed. Serve warm or at room temperature.

HONEY CHOPS WITH GLAZED CARROTS

These tasty, sticky chops are very quick and easy to prepare and grill. Serve them with herbed mashed potatoes or french fries.

Serves 4

4 pork loin chops

¼ cup butter

2 tablespoons clear honey

1 tablespoon tomato paste

For the carrots

1 pound carrots

1 tablespoon butter

1 tablespoon light brown sugar

1 tablespoon sesame seeds, to serve

VARIATION

Use mustard instead of tomato paste, if you prefer. A whole-grain mustard would be ideal.

Prepare the carrots: cut them into matchsticks, put them in a saucepan and add just enough cold water to cover. Stir in the butter and brown sugar and bring to a boil. Lower the heat and simmer for 15–20 minutes, until most of the liquid has boiled away. Preheat the broiler to high.

Line the broiler pan with foil and arrange the pork chops on the top tray. Beat the butter and honey together and gradually beat in the tomato paste to make a smooth paste.

Spread half the honey paste over the chops and broil for 5 minutes, until browned. Turn the chops over, spread them with the remaining honey paste and broil the second side for 5 minutes or until the meat is cooked through. Sprinkle the sesame seeds over the carrots and serve with the chops.

CHINESE HONEY-GLAZED CHICKEN WINGS

The honey makes these gloriously sticky, so make sure you provide finger bowls and paper napkins.

Serves 4

12 chicken wings

3 garlic cloves, crushed

1½-inch piece fresh
  ginger, grated

juice of 1 large lemon

3 tablespoons soy sauce

3 tablespoons clear honey

½ teaspoon chili powder

⅔ cup chicken stock

salt and ground black pepper

lemon wedges, to garnish

COOK'S TIP

*Use the wing tips from the
pieces of chicken to make the
stock, if desired. Add a slice
each of carrot and onion, and
a bay leaf.*

Remove the wing tips and cut each wing into two joints. Mix the garlic, ginger, lemon juice, soy sauce, honey, chili powder and seasoning in a dish. Add the chicken pieces, turning to coat them. Cover with plastic wrap and marinate overnight.

Preheat the oven to 425°F. Lift the wings out of the marinade and arrange them in a single layer in a roasting pan. Bake for 20–25 minutes, basting at least twice with the marinade during cooking.

Place the wings on a plate and keep them hot. Add the stock to the marinade in the roasting pan, and bring to a boil. Cook until syrupy, then spoon a little over the wings. Serve garnished with the lemon wedges.

AVOCADO SALAD WITH HONEY DRESSING

This salad, with its delicate honey and mint dressing, makes an ideal appetizer for a summer dinner party.

Serves 6

1 pink grapefruit
1 yellow grapefruit
1 cantaloupe, halved
  and seeded
2 large, ripe but firm avocados
2 tablespoons fresh lemon juice
2 tablespoons vegetable oil
1 tablespoon clear honey
3 tablespoons chopped fresh mint
salt and ground black pepper
fresh mint leaves, to garnish

COOK'S TIP

If you do not have a melon baller, cut the melon into wedges, the same size as the grapefruit segments. Do the same with the avocados.

Peel and segment both grapefruit, using a sharp knife, and cut between the membranes. Put the segments in a bowl. With a melon baller, scoop out balls from the melon flesh and add them to the grapefruit. Chill the fruit for at least 30 minutes.

Cut the avocados in half and discard the pits. Peel off the skins, then cut the flesh into small pieces. Place in a bowl, add the lemon juice and toss to coat well. Using a slotted spoon, add the avocado to the grapefruit mixture. Reserve the remaining lemon juice.

Make the dressing by whisking the oil into the reserved lemon juice. Stir in the honey and chopped mint, with salt and pepper to taste. Pour the dressing over the fruit and toss gently. Garnish with mint leaves and serve.

PINEAPPLE, HONEY AND MINT CHUTNEY

This tasty fruit chutney goes particularly well with pork or lamb dishes.

Makes 3 cups

1 cup raspberry vinegar

1 cup dry white wine

1 small pineapple, peeled
  and chopped

2 oranges, peeled and chopped

1 apple, peeled and chopped

1 red bell pepper, seeded and diced

2 small onions, finely chopped

¼ cup honey

pinch of salt

1 clove

4 black peppercorns

2 tablespoons chopped fresh mint

In a saucepan, combine the vinegar and wine and bring to a boil. Boil for 3 minutes. Add the remaining ingredients, except the mint, and stir to blend. Simmer gently for about 30 minutes, stirring occasionally. Transfer to a strainer set over a bowl and drain, pressing down to extract the liquid. Remove and discard the clove and peppercorns. Set the fruit mixture aside.

Return the strained juice to the pan and boil until reduced by two-thirds. Pour it over the fruit mixture.

Stir in the mint. Let the chutney stand for 6–8 hours before serving.

17

SPICED SALMON AND HONEY STIR-FRY

Marinating the salmon with honey allows all the flavors to develop, and the lime tenderizes the fish beautifully, so it needs very little stir-frying – be careful not to overcook it.

Serves 4

4 salmon steaks, 8 ounces each
4 whole star anise
2 lemongrass stalks, sliced
juice of 3 limes
finely grated rind of 3 limes
2 tablespoons clear honey
2 tablespoons grapeseed oil
salt and ground black pepper
lime wedges, to garnish

COOK'S TIP
Sprinkle about 1 teaspoon salt on the cutting board before skinning the salmon and it will be much easier to handle and less likely to slide.

Remove the middle bone from each salmon steak to make two strips from each. Remove the skin and slice the salmon diagonally into pieces.

Roughly crush the star anise in a mortar with a pestle. Place in a non-metallic dish, with the lemongrass, lime juice and rind and honey. Mix well. Add the salmon, turning to coat the pieces in the mixture. Season well with salt and pepper, cover and chill overnight.

Lift the pieces of salmon out of the marinade and pat them dry with paper towels. Reserve the marinade.

Heat a wok, then add the oil. When the oil is hot, add the salmon and stir-fry, stirring constantly until cooked. Increase the heat, pour in the marinade and bring to a boil. Serve immediately, garnished with the lime wedges.

HONEY-GLAZED CARROTS

Honey accentuates the natural sweetness of the carrots, and orange juice adds a delicious piquancy.

Serves 6

*1 pound baby carrots, trimmed
and peeled*

3 tablespoons butter or margarine

2 tablespoons honey

2 tablespoons fresh orange juice

*8 ounces scallions, cut diagonally
into 1-inch lengths*

salt and ground black pepper

Cook the carrots in boiling salted water or steam them for 10 minutes until just tender. Drain if necessary.

In a frying pan, melt the butter with the honey and orange juice, stirring until the mixture is smooth and well combined.

Add the carrots and scallions to the pan. Cook for about 5 minutes over medium heat, stirring occasionally, until the vegetables are heated through and glazed. Season to taste before serving.

Fish, Poultry, Meat and Main Dishes

Although we tend to think of honey in terms of sweet dishes, it makes an admirable addition to all sorts of savories, including roast ham, pan-fried calf's liver and glazed poultry. Try the fruit and honey relish – it's perfect with pork.

HONEYED SALMON FILLETS

Honey, soy sauce and lime juice combine to make a magical marinade for grilled salmon.

Serves 6

2 pounds salmon fillet,
*   cut in 6 pieces*
½ cup clear honey
¼ cup soy sauce
juice of 2 limes
1 tablespoon sesame oil
¼ teaspoon crushed dried chili
¼ teaspoon crushed
*   black peppercorns*
lettuce, to garnish

COOK'S TIP

The acid in the citrus juice begins to "cook" the fish, so it is only necessary to broil the pieces on one side.

Place the salmon pieces skin-side down in a baking dish large enough to hold them all in a single layer.

Combine the honey, soy sauce, lime juice, sesame oil, crushed chili and peppercorns in a bowl. Mix well. Pour the mixture over the fish. Cover and marinate for 30 minutes.

Preheat the broiler. Lift the fish out of the marinade and arrange on the top tray of the broiler pan, skin-side down. Grill about 3 inches from the heat for 6–8 minutes or until the fish flakes easily. Garnish with lettuce.

HONEY-ROAST CHICKEN

A honey glaze not only gives roast chicken a glorious golden skin – it also improves the flavor.

Serves 4

3–3½ pound chicken

2 tablespoons clear honey

1 tablespoon brandy

1½ tablespoons flour

⅔ cup chicken stock

green beans, to serve

For the stuffing

4 strips bacon, chopped

2 shallots chopped

¾ cup button
  mushrooms, quartered

1 tablespoon butter or margarine

2 thick slices white bread, diced

1 tablespoon chopped fresh parsley

salt and ground black pepper

Make the stuffing. Heat the bacon in a frying pan until the fat runs, then add the shallots and mushrooms and fry over medium heat for 5 minutes. With a slotted spoon, transfer the bacon and vegetables to a bowl.

Pour off all but 2 tablespoons bacon fat from the pan. Add the butter. When it is hot, fry the diced bread until golden brown. Add it to the bacon mixture, stir in the parsley and add salt and pepper to taste. Let cool. Preheat the oven to 350°F.

Pack the stuffing into the body cavity of the chicken. Truss it neatly, then place it in a roasting pan.

Mix the honey with the brandy. Brush half the mixture over the chicken. Roast for 1¼–1½ hours, until the chicken is thoroughly cooked. Baste the chicken frequently with the remaining honey mixture during roasting.

Transfer the chicken to a warmed serving platter. Cover with foil and set aside. Strain the cooking juices into a pitcher. Skim off the surface fat.

Stir the flour into the sediment in the roasting tin. Add the remaining degreased cooking juices and the stock. Boil rapidly until the gravy has thickened, stirring constantly. Pour the gravy into a warmed sauceboat and serve with the chicken and lightly cooked green beans.

COOK'S TIP
Use smoked bacon for the stuffing.

HONEY AND ORANGE-GLAZED CHICKEN

Try orange-blossom honey for this tasty glaze. It makes a perfect partner for chicken and oranges.

Serves 4

4 chicken breasts, 6 ounces each,
   boned and skinned

1 tablespoon oil

4 scallions, chopped

1 garlic clove, crushed

3 tablespoons clear honey

¼ cup fresh orange juice

1 orange, peeled and segmented

2 tablespoons soy sauce

fresh lemon balm or flat-leaf parsley
   sprigs, to garnish

baked potatoes and salad, to serve

VARIATION

The sauce is equally good when served with pork chops.

Preheat the oven to 375°F. Place the chicken breasts in a shallow roasting pan and set aside.

Heat the oil in a small pan. Fry the scallions and crushed garlic for 2 minutes, until softened. Add the honey, orange juice, orange segments and soy sauce to the pan, stirring well until the honey has dissolved.

Pour the mixture over the chicken and bake, uncovered, for 45 minutes, basting once or twice, until the chicken is cooked through. Serve on plates, garnished with lemon balm or parsley, accompanied by baked potatoes and a fresh salad.

HONEY-COATED DUCK

Crisp honey-glazed duck in a mandarin sauce, served with stir-fried vegetables, makes a tasty dish.

Serves 4

4 duck legs or boneless breasts

2 tablespoons light soy sauce

3 tablespoons clear honey

1 tablespoon sesame seeds

4 mandarin oranges

1 teaspoon cornstarch

salt and ground black pepper

COOK'S TIP

Pricking the duck skin all over allows much of the fat to drain away, but the meat remains deliciously moist.

Preheat the oven to 350°F. Prick the duck skin all over with a fork. If using breasts of duck, slash the skin diagonally at intervals with a sharp knife.

Place the duck legs on a rack in a roasting pan and roast for 1 hour. Meanwhile, mix 1 tablespoon of the soy sauce with 2 tablespoons of the honey. Remove the duck from the oven, brush with the honey mixture and sprinkle with the sesame seeds. Roast for 15–20 more minutes, until golden brown.

Grate the rind from 1 mandarin and squeeze the juice from 2 of them. Mix the rind and juice in a small pan. Stir in the cornstarch, then the remaining soy sauce and honey. Heat, stirring, until the sauce thickens and clears. Add salt and pepper to taste, and keep hot. Peel and slice the remaining mandarins. Serve the duck with the mandarin slices and the sauce.

PORK WITH FRUIT AND HONEY RELISH

Roasted chili, nectarines and honey make a harmonious mixture to serve with grilled pork chops.

Serves 4

1 cup fresh orange juice

3 tablespoons olive oil

2 garlic cloves, crushed

1 teaspoon ground cumin

*1 tablespoon coarsely ground
    black pepper*

*8 pork loin chops, about ¾-inch
    thick, well trimmed*

salt

*nectarine slices, lettuce and chervil
    sprigs, to garnish*

For the relish

1 small fresh green chili

2 tablespoons clear honey

juice of ½ lemon

1 cup chicken stock

2 nectarines, pitted and chopped

1 garlic clove, crushed

½ onion, finely chopped

*1 teaspoon finely chopped
    fresh ginger*

¼ teaspoon salt

1 tablespoon chopped fresh cilantro

Make the relish. Roast the chili over a gas flame, holding it with tongs, until charred on all sides. (Alternatively, char the skin under the broiler.) Set aside to cool for 5 minutes. Carefully rub the charred skin off the chili. Chop the chili finely, discarding the seeds if you prefer a milder flavor, and put it in a saucepan. Add all the remaining ingredients except the cilantro. Bring to a boil, then lower the heat and simmer, stirring occasionally, for about 30 minutes. Stir in the cilantro and set aside.

In a small bowl, combine the orange juice, oil, garlic, cumin and pepper. Stir to mix. Arrange the pork chops in a shallow dish large enough to hold them all in a single layer. Pour on the orange juice mixture and turn to coat. Cover and let stand for at least 1 hour, or refrigerate overnight.

Lift the pork chops out of the marinade and pat them dry with paper towels.

Heat a ridged grill pan. When hot, add the pork chops and cook for 5 minutes, until browned. Turn and cook the other side for 10 minutes or more, until cooked through. Serve immediately, with the relish. Garnish with nectarine slices, lettuce and chervil.

HONEY-ROAST HAM

A honey-glazed ham makes the perfect centerpiece for a celebratory meal, whether you serve it hot or cold. Cumberland sauce is the perfect accompaniment.

Serves 8–10

4½ pounds ham

1 onion, quartered

cloves

2 bay leaves

few black peppercorns

pared rind of ½ orange

small piece fresh ginger

½ cinnamon stick

few parsley stalks

cranberry jelly, apple sauce or
*   Cumberland sauce, to serve*

For the glaze

cloves

6 tablespoons clear honey

2 tablespoons whole-grain mustard

Weigh the ham and calculate the cooking time at 20 minutes per pound, plus 20 minutes extra. Place the ham in a large pan and cover with cold water. Bring to a boil and remove from the heat. Pour off the water, rinse the pan and replace the ham. Cover it with cold water and add the onion quarters, studded with cloves, and the bay leaves, peppercorns, orange rind, ginger, cinnamon and parsley stalks. Bring slowly to a boil, cover the pan and lower the heat. Simmer for the calculated cooking time less 15 minutes. In the case of a ham weighing 4½ pounds, this would be 1 hour, 35 minutes.

Lift the ham out of the pan (reserve the stock for soups, casseroles and sauces) and let it cool slightly. Cut off the rind from the ham as evenly as possible and score the fat in a diamond pattern with a sharp knife. Preheat the oven to 350°F.

Press cloves into the scored ham fat at intervals. Mix the honey and mustard in a bowl and spread it over the skin. Wrap the ham in foil, leaving only the glazed area uncovered.

Place the ham, glazed-side up, in a roasting pan and bake for about 15 minutes. Serve hot or cold, with cranberry jelly, apple sauce or its traditional accompaniment, Cumberland sauce.

SAUTEED LIVER WITH HONEY

A wonderful sweet-and-sour sauce, made from honey and sherry vinegar, proves the perfect foil for tender calves' liver in this recipe from France.

Serves 4

4 slices calves' liver,
   6 ounces each
flour, for dusting
2 tablespoons butter
2 tablespoons vegetable oil
2 tablespoons sherry vinegar or red
   wine vinegar
2–3 tablespoons chicken stock
1 tablespoon clear honey
salt and ground black pepper
watercress sprigs, to garnish

COOK'S TIP
The calves' liver should be cut about ½ inch thick. Cook it until it is well browned on the outside but still slightly pink in the center.

Wipe the liver slices with damp paper towels, then season both sides with a little salt and pepper and dust the slices lightly with flour, shaking off any excess.

In a large heavy frying pan, melt half of the butter with the oil over high heat and swirl to blend.

Add the liver slices to the pan and cook for 1–2 minutes, until browned on one side, then turn and cook for 1 more minute. Transfer to heated plates and keep hot.

Stir the vinegar, stock and honey into the pan. Boil for 1 minute, stirring constantly, then add the remaining butter, stirring until melted and smooth. Spoon the sauce over the liver slices, garnish with watercress sprigs and serve.

HONEY-GLAZED LAMB

Lemon and honey is a classic combination, perfect for both savory and sweet dishes.

Serves 4

1 pound boneless lean lamb

1 tablespoon grapeseed oil

6 ounces snow peas, trimmed

3 scallions, sliced

2 tablespoons clear honey

juice of ½ lemon

2 tablespoons chopped fresh cilantro

1 tablespoon sesame seeds

salt and ground black pepper

cilantro sprigs, to garnish

lemon slices, to serve

COOK'S TIP

Use stir-fry oil for frying, if desired. A blend of sunflower oil and sesame oil is full of flavor and does not readily burn at high temperatures.

Using a sharp knife, cut the lamb into thin strips. Heat a wok, then add the oil. When the oil is hot, stir-fry the lamb until browned all over. Remove from the wok with a slotted spoon and keep hot.

Add the snowpeas and scallions to the oil remaining in the hot wok and stir-fry for 30 seconds.

Return the lamb to the wok and add the honey, lemon juice, cilantro and sesame seeds, with plenty of salt and pepper. Bring to a boil and bubble for 1 minute until the lamb is coated in the honey mixture. Serve immediately with lemon slices and garnished with cilantro sprigs.

Breads, Cakes and Bars

One of honey's many attributes is its ability to absorb moisture, so cakes and cookies made with honey remain moist and keep for a longer time than those made with sugar. They also taste superb, so you may not get the opportunity to prove the point.

WALNUT AND HONEY BREAD

Honey gives this nutty bread a superb flavor that intensifies the longer you keep it.

Makes 1 loaf

2½ cups whole-wheat flour

1 cup white flour

2 teaspoons salt

¼-ounce envelope
*   dried yeast*

2 tablespoons clear honey

2 cups warm water

1¼ cups walnut pieces, plus extra to
*   decorate*

1 beaten egg, to glaze

COOK'S TIP

Flours vary in their
absorbency, so you may need to
add a little more water when
making the dough.

Combine the flours, salt and yeast in a bowl. Make a well in the center. Dissolve the honey in the water, then pour the mixture into the well and stir to obtain a smooth dough. Add more flour if the dough is too sticky and use your hands if the dough becomes too stiff to stir. Knead the dough, adding flour if necessary, until smooth and elastic. Knead in the walnuts.

Shape the walnut and honey dough into a round loaf and place it on a greased baking sheet. Press in more walnut pieces to decorate the top. Cover loosely and let rise in a warm place until doubled in size.

Preheat the oven to 425°F. Score the top of the loaf with a sharp knife. Brush with the egg. Bake for 15 minutes, then lower the oven temperature to 375°F and bake for 40 minutes or until the bottom of the loaf sounds hollow when tapped. Cool on a wire rack.

HONEY GRAIN BREAD

This is a particularly tasty loaf, with a subtle hint of honey. Serve toasted, spread with butter and honey.

Makes 2 loaves

generous ¾ cup rolled oats

2½ cups milk

¼ cup sunflower oil

⅓ cup light brown sugar

2 tablespoons clear honey

4 cups white flour

2 cups soy flour

3 cups whole-wheat flour

½ cup wheat germ

2 teaspoon salt

¼-ounce envelope dried yeast

2 eggs, lightly beaten

Put the oats in a large bowl. Heat the milk in a saucepan until just below boiling point, then pour it over the oats. Stir in the oil, sugar and honey. Cool the mixture until it is just warm.

Combine the flours, wheatgerm, salt and yeast in a large mixing bowl. Add the oat mixture and eggs and mix to a rough dough. Knead on a lightly floured surface for about 10 minutes, until smooth and elastic.

Grease two 9 x 5-inch loaf tins. Divide the dough into four equal pieces and roll each to a rope slightly longer than the tin and about 1½ inches thick. Twist the ropes together in pairs and place in the tins. Cover loosely and let rise in a warm place until doubled in size.

Preheat the oven to 425°F. Bake the honey loaves for 30–35 minutes, then remove from the pans and cool on a wire rack.

COOK'S TIP

To test the loaves, hold each upside down in an oven-gloved hand. Make a fist of your other hand and tap gently on the bottom of the loaf. If it sounds hollow, the loaf is done.

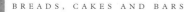

YOGURT HONEY MUFFINS

There's quite a lot of honey in these muffins, so choose a light subtle-flavored variety such as acacia.

Makes 12

¼ cup butter

5 tablespoons clear honey

1 cup plain yogurt

1 egg

grated rind of 1 lemon

¼ cup fresh lemon juice

1 cup flour

1 cup whole-wheat flour

½ teaspoon baking soda

pinch of grated nutmeg

Preheat the oven to 375°F. Grease a 12-cup muffin tin or use paper liners. Melt the butter with the honey in a saucepan. Remove from the heat and set aside to cool slightly.

In a bowl, whisk together the yogurt, egg, lemon rind and juice. Add the butter and honey mixture. Mix well.

Sift the dry ingredients into a second bowl, then fold them into the yogurt mixture until just blended.

Fill the prepared muffin cups two-thirds full. Bake for 20–25 minutes, or until the tops spring back when lightly touched. Let cool in the tin for 5 minutes before turning the muffins out onto a wire rack. Serve warm or at room temperature.

VARIATION

For a more substantial muffin, fold in ½ cup chopped walnuts with the flour.

36

ORANGE HONEY BREAD

Honey improves the keeping quality of cakes and breads, but this is so delicious that you are unlikely to be able to put the theory to the test.

Makes 1 loaf
2½ cups flour
2½ teaspoons baking powder
½ teaspoon baking soda
½ teaspoon salt
2 tablespoons margarine
1 cup clear honey
1 egg, lightly beaten
¼ cup grated orange rind
¾ cup fresh
    orange juice
¾ cup chopped walnuts

Preheat the oven to 325°F. Grease a 9 x 5-inch loaf pan and line the base with non-stick baking paper. Sift the flour, baking powder, baking soda and salt together.

Cream the margarine in a mixing bowl until soft. Stir in the honey until well mixed, then stir in the lightly beaten egg. Add the orange rind and stir to combine thoroughly.

Fold the flour mixture into the honey and egg mixture in three batches, alternating with the orange juice. Stir in the walnuts.

Pour into the prepared pan and bake for about 1 hour or until a cake tester inserted in the center of the loaf comes out clean. Let stand for 10 minutes before turning out onto a wire rack to cool.

BANANA AND HONEY LOAF

For the best flavor and a really good, moist texture, use very ripe bananas for this cake.

Makes 1 loaf

⅔ cup whole-wheat flour

⅔ cup flour

1 teaspoon baking powder

1 teaspoon pumpkin pie spice

3 tablespoons chopped
   hazelnuts, toasted

2 large ripe bananas

1 egg

2 tablespoons sunflower oil, plus extra
   for greasing

2 tablespoons clear honey

grated rind and juice of 1 orange

4 orange slices, halved, and
   1 teaspoon confectioners' sugar,
   to decorate

COOK'S TIP

If you plan to keep the loaf for more than three days, omit the orange slices. Instead, brush with honey and sprinkle with slivered hazelnuts.

Preheat the oven to 350°F. Brush a 9 x 5-inch loaf pan lightly with oil and line the base with non-stick baking paper.

Sift the flours with the baking powder and spice into a large bowl, adding any bran that remains in the sieve. Stir in the hazelnuts.

Mash the bananas in a mixing bowl. Beat in the egg, oil, honey, orange rind and juice. Add to the dry ingredients and mix well.

Spoon the mixture into the prepared pan and smooth the surface. Bake for 40–45 minutes or until firm and golden brown. Turn out onto a wire rack to cool. Preheat the broiler.

Sprinkle the orange slices with the confectioners' sugar and broil until golden. Cool slightly, then use to decorate the loaf.

HONEY-GLAZED APPLE PIE

Here's your chance to experiment with a honey flavor that you feel best suits your chosen apples. Try a heather honey, perhaps, or a Jamaican tropical flower variety.

Serves 8

2½ cups flour

½ teaspoon salt

½ cup chilled unsalted butter, diced

¼ cup chilled vegetable
   shortening, diced

5–6 tablespoons ice water

3–3½ pounds firm apples, peeled,
   cored and sliced

¼ cup sugar

2 teaspoons ground cinnamon

grated rind and juice of 1 lemon

2 tablespoons butter for the apples,
   diced

2–3 tablespoons clear honey, heated

Sift the flour and salt into a bowl. Rub in the fats until the mixture resembles coarse bread crumbs. Stir in enough ice water to moisten the dry ingredients, then gather together to make a ball. Wrap the pastry and chill for 30 minutes. Preheat the oven to 400°F.

Put the apple slices, sugar, cinnamon, lemon rind and juice in a bowl and toss together well.

Roll out the pastry to a 12-inch round. Fit the pastry in the pie dish so that the excess dough overhangs the edges. Fill with the apple mixture, then fold in the edges, crimping them loosely to make a decorative border. Dot the apples with the diced butter.

Bake the pie for 45 minutes, until the pastry is golden and the apples tender. Remove from the oven and brush the honey over the apples to glaze.

PECAN AND HONEY BARS

Honey and nuts go very well together, as this recipe proves. If you can't find pecans, use walnuts instead.

Makes 36 squares

2 cups flour

pinch of salt

½ cup sugar

1 cup butter or
  margarine, diced

1 egg

finely grated rind of 1 lemon

For the topping

¾ cup butter

¼ cup clear honey

¼ cup sugar

¾ cup dark
  brown sugar

5 tablespoons whipping cream

4 cups pecans

Lightly grease a 14 x 11-inch jelly roll pan. Sift the flour and salt into a bowl. Stir in the sugar, then rub in the fat until the mixture resembles coarse bread crumbs. Blend in the egg and lemon rind.

Press the mixture into the prepared pan and prick the pastry all over with a fork. Chill for 10 minutes. Preheat the oven to 375°F.

Bake the pastry for 15 minutes, then remove the pan from the oven (leave the oven on). Heat the butter, honey and sugars in a pan until melted, then bring to a boil and boil without stirring for 2 minutes. Remove from the heat and stir in the cream and pecans. Pour over the base, return the tin to the oven and bake for 25 minutes. Cool in the pan.

Run a knife around the pastry edge, invert onto a baking sheet, place another sheet on top and invert again. Cut into squares for serving.

BAKLAVA

In Greece, the wonderful herb honey from Mount Hymettus would be used for this sweet filo pastry. Dark, clear and slightly thick, it owes its flavor to thyme and marjoram blossoms.

Makes 10 pieces

6 tablespoons butter, melted

6 large sheets filo pastry

2 cups chopped mixed nuts (such as almonds, pistachios, hazelnuts and walnuts)

1 cup fresh bread crumbs

1 teaspoon ground cinnamon

1 teaspoon pumpkin pie spice

½ teaspoon grated nutmeg

1 cup clear honey

¼ cup lemon juice

Preheat the oven to 350°F. Butter an 11 x 7-inch pan. Unroll the filo pastry, brush one sheet with melted butter and use it to line the pan, easing it carefully up the sides. Repeat the process with two more sheets of filo, easing the pastry into the corners and letting the edges overhang the pan.

Mix the nuts, bread crumbs and spices in a bowl and spoon this mixture evenly into the lined pan.

Cut the remaining three sheets of filo pastry in half horizontally and brush each one with a little butter. Layer half the pieces of filo on top of the filling and fold in any overhanging edges. Top with the remaining buttered filo. With a sharp knife, mark the baklava diagonally into diamonds. Bake for about 30 minutes, until the pastry is golden.

Meanwhile, heat the honey and lemon juice gently in a pan. When the baklava is cooked, remove it from the oven and pour the syrup over it while still warm. Let cool completely, then cut into diamonds, following the markings in the pastry, and serve.

COOK'S TIP

Filo pastry dries out very quickly, so keep any pieces not being used covered with a lightly dampened dish towel.

GREEK HONEY AND LEMON CAKE

To be authentic, you should use a Greek blossom honey, such as Hymettus, for this cake, but clear clover honey would also be good.

Makes 16 slices

3 tablespoons butter or margarine

¼ cup clear honey

finely grated rind and juice of
   1 lemon

⅔ cup milk

1¼ cups flour

1½ teaspoons baking powder

½ teaspoon grated nutmeg

¼ cup semolina

2 egg whites

2 teaspoons sesame seeds

COOK'S TIP

Use a clean metal spoon and a figure-eight action when you fold the egg whites into the cake mixture.

Preheat the oven to 400°F. Grease a 7½-inch square deep cake pan and line the base with non-stick baking paper. Mix the butter with 3 tablespoons of the honey in a saucepan and heat gently until melted. Reserve 1 tablespoon lemon juice. Stir the rest into the honey mixture, with the lemon rind and milk.

Sift the flour, baking powder and nutmeg into a bowl, then beat in the honey mixture with the semolina. Whisk the egg whites until they form soft peaks, then fold them evenly into the mixture.

Spoon the mixture into the pan and sprinkle with sesame seeds. Bake for 25–30 minutes, until golden brown. Mix the reserved honey and lemon juice and drizzle over the cake while warm. Cool in the pan, then cut into fingers.

HONEY APPLE CAKE

Honey makes this a moist cake. Instead of using apples, try making it with pears for a change.

Serves 8

½ cup butter or margarine

¾ cup clear honey

3 eggs, beaten

1½ cups flour

1½ cups whole-wheat flour

½ teaspoon salt

½ teaspoon baking soda

few drops vanilla

1 large apple

3–4 tablespoons milk or apple juice

few apple slices and 2–3 tablespoons
   brown sugar, for topping

butter, to serve (optional)

COOK'S TIP

Substituting honey for some or all of the sugar in a creamed cake mixture like this one gives a delicious flavor.

Preheat the oven to 350°F. Grease a 7-inch square or 8-inch round cake pan. Cream the butter and honey until soft and pale. Beat in the eggs, then fold in the dry ingredients and vanilla.

Peel, core and grate the apple. Stir it into the mixture, with enough of the milk or apple juice to give a soft dropping consistency. Spoon the mixture into the pan and smooth the surface.

Bake for 30 minutes, then arrange the apple slices on the top and sprinkle generously with brown sugar. Continue cooking for 30 more minutes, or until the cake is just firm to the touch.

Turn off the heat and let the cake cool in the oven. Remove from the pan before it is completely cold and wrap in foil to store. Serve sliced, with butter or simply on its own.

Cold Desserts

Some of the simplest and most delicious desserts
are based on honey. Whether you prefer
fresh fruit with a honey dip, a creamy ice cream
or a wonderful whiskey-flavored treat, honey
ensures the sweet taste of success.

HONEY AND MANGO CHEESECAKE

Use a fragrant citrus honey to complement the mango and lime in this exotic cheesecake.

Serves 4

3 tablespoons butter or margarine,
    softened

2 tablespoons clear honey

2 cups oatmeal

1 large ripe mango, peeled, pitted
    and roughly chopped

1¼ cups cream cheese

¾ cup plain yogurt

finely grated rind of 1 small lime

3 tablespoons apple juice

4 teaspoons powdered gelatin

fresh mango and lime slices, to
    decorate

VARIATION

Use drained canned mango slices instead of fresh, if you prefer, but add a few drops of fresh lime juice to counteract the sweetness.

Preheat the oven to 400°F. Cream the butter with the honey in a bowl, then stir in the oatmeal. Press the mixture into the base of an 8-inch springform cake pan. Bake for 12–15 minutes, until lightly browned. Cool.

Place the chopped mango, cheese, yogurt and lime rind in a food processor or blender and process until smooth.

Put the apple juice in a small heatproof bowl and sprinkle the gelatine on top. When spongy, set over simmering water and stir until the gelatin has dissolved. Stir into the cheese mixture.

Pour the filling over the cheesecake base and chill until set, then remove from the pan and place on a serving plate. Decorate the top with the mango and lime slices.

VANILLA AND HONEY ICE CREAM

Honey ice cream is delicious. Pour a little Drambuie or other whiskey and honey liqueur over the top for an extra-special treat.

Serves 4

1 cup buttermilk

¼ cup heavy cream

1 vanilla pod or
   ½ teaspoon vanilla extract

2 eggs

2 tablespoons clear honey

VARIATION

Ice cream can be used as a base for other flavors: stir in puréed or chopped fruit, dissolved instant coffee or citrus rind, or coat the frozen roll in a layer of dry, shredded coconut or chopped nuts.

Place the buttermilk and cream in a pan. At this point, add the vanilla pod, if using, and heat gently until the mixture is almost boiling. Remove the pod. Put the eggs in a heatproof bowl. Place over a pan of hot water and whisk until pale and thick. Pour in the heated buttermilk mixture in a thin stream, whisking constantly. Continue whisking over the hot water until the mixture thickens slightly.

Whisk in the honey and, if using vanilla extract, add at this point. Spoon the mixture into a freezer container and freeze until the mixture is firm enough to hold its shape, then spoon it onto a sheet of non-stick baking paper. Form the semi-frozen ice cream into a sausage shape and roll it up in the paper. Freeze again until firm. Slice the ice cream, giving it a few minutes to soften before serving.

Banana-honey Yogurt Ice

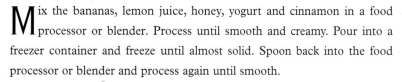

Invented for dieters, this honey ice is a winner with everyone.

Serves 4–6

4 ripe bananas, roughly chopped

1 tablespoon lemon juice

2 tablespoons clear honey

1 cup thick plain yogurt

½ teaspoon ground cinnamon

cookies, slivered hazelnuts, and

banana slices, to serve

Mix the bananas, lemon juice, honey, yogurt and cinnamon in a food processor or blender. Process until smooth and creamy. Pour into a freezer container and freeze until almost solid. Spoon back into the food processor or blender and process again until smooth.

Return the mixture to the container and freeze again until firm. Let soften at room temperature for 15 minutes, then serve in scoops with cookies, slivered hazelnuts and banana slices.

Strawberry and Honey Pashka

This version of a traditional Russian dessert of cream cheese flavoured with honey is ideal for dinner parties – make it a day or two in advance for best results.

Serves 4

350g/12oz/1½ cups cottage cheese or
*   cream cheese*
175ml/6fl oz/¾ cup natural yogurt
30ml/2 tbsp clear honey
2.5ml/½ tsp rosewater
450g/1lb/2½ cups strawberries
handful of scented pink rose petals, to
*   decorate*

If using cottage cheese, drain off any liquid and pour the cheese into a sieve. Use a wooden spoon to rub it through the sieve into a mixing bowl. If using cream cheese, simply beat it lightly to soften. Stir in the yogurt, honey and rosewater.

Chop about half the strawberries and stir them into the cheese mixture.

Line a new, clean flowerpot or a sieve with fine cheesecloth and tip the cheese mixture into it. Leave it to drain over a mixing bowl for several hours, or overnight.

Invert the flowerpot or sieve on to a serving plate, turn out the pashka and remove the cheesecloth. Slice the reserved strawberries in half, leaving the greenery in place, and use with the rose petals to decorate the pashka.

Cook's Tip

A flowerpot shape is traditional for pashka, but you could make it in any shape – the small porcelain heart-shape moulds with draining holes used for coeurs à la crème make a pretty alternative.

ORANGE, HONEY AND MINT TERRINE

Orange blossom honey is the best choice for this refreshing dessert. It is ideal for serving after a rich meal as it is a good palate cleanser.

Serves 6

8–10 oranges

2½ cups fresh
  orange juice

2 tablespoons clear honey

4 teaspoons agar-agar

3 tablespoons fresh mint, chopped

mint leaves, to decorate (optional)

COOK'S TIP

Agar-agar is the vegetarian's preferred setting agent as it comes from a non-meat source. If you prefer, use 1 envelope of powdered gelatin, softened in 2 tablespoons cold water.

Grate the rind from 2 oranges and set aside. Peel all the oranges, then slice thinly, working over a pan to catch any juice. Set the slices aside.

Add the measured orange juice to the orange juice in the pan, with the honey, reserved rind and agar-agar. Stir the mixture over low heat until the honey and agar-agar have dissolved.

Pack the orange slices into a 2¼-pound loaf pan, sprinkling the mint between the layers. Slowly pour over the hot orange juice. Tap the pan lightly so that all the juice settles. Chill the terrine for several hours or overnight, until it is quite firm. When ready to serve, dip the pan briefly into very hot water and turn the terrine out onto a wet platter. Decorate with more mint leaves, if desired. Serve cut into thick slices.

GINGER AND HONEY WINTER FRUITS

A compote of dried fruit flavored with honey is equally tasty as a dessert or breakfast dish. Serve it with yogurt or cream.

Serves 4

1 lemon

4 green cardamom pods

1 cinnamon stick

⅔ cup clear honey

2 tablespoons ginger syrup, from the jar

2½ cups assorted dried fruits

1-inch piece fresh ginger

1 orange, peeled and segmented

VARIATION

Omit the ginger syrup and use 2 tablespoons rosewater instead. Add ½ cup blanched almonds as well.

Thinly pare 2 strips of rind from the lemon. Lightly crush the cardamom pods with the back of a heavy-bladed knife. Place the lemon rind, cardamoms, cinnamon stick, honey and ginger syrup in a heavy saucepan. Pour in ¼ cup water and add the dried fruit. Bring to a boil, then lower the heat and simmer for 10 minutes. Pour into a serving bowl. Set aside until cool.

Chop the ginger finely and stir it into the fruit salad, with the orange segments. Cover and chill until ready to serve.

GRAPE AND HONEY WHIP

Frosted grapes add the finishing touches to this simple dessert, which is sweetened with clear honey.

Serves 4

115g/4oz/1 cup black or green
*   seedless grapes, plus 4 sprigs*
2 egg whites
15ml/1 tbsp granulated sugar
finely grated rind and juice of
*   ½ lemon*
250g/9oz/1 cup cream cheese
45ml/3 tbsp clear honey
30ml/2 tbsp brandy (optional)

VARIATION
Instead of brandy, use a honey-
based liqueur such as Irish
Mist, made from Irish whiskey,
heather honey and herbs.

Brush the sprigs of grapes lightly with some of the egg whites and sprinkle with sugar to coat. Leave to dry.

Pour the lemon juice into a bowl and stir in the rind, cheese, honey and brandy, if using. Chop the remaining grapes and stir them in.

Whisk the remaining egg whites until they are stiff enough to hold soft peaks. Fold them into the grape mixture, then spoon into serving glasses. Top with the sugar-frosted grapes and serve chilled.

FRUDITÉS WITH HONEY DIP

Some of the simplest desserts are also the most delectable. This takes only minutes to make but tastes absolutely wonderful, making use of the classic honey and yogurt combination.

Serves 4

*250ml/8fl oz/1 cup thick natural
   yogurt*
45ml/3 tbsp clear honey
*selection of fresh fruit for dipping
   (such as apples, pears, tangerines,
   grapes, figs, cherries, strawberries
   and kiwi fruit)*

VARIATION

Add a few langues de chat *or
other dessert biscuits, such as
sponge fingers, to the platter.
Children like the yogurt dip
served on its own, with sliced
bananas stirred in.*

Place the yogurt in a dish, beat until smooth, then stir in the honey, swirling it to create a marbled effect.

Cut the fruit into wedges or bite-size pieces, or leave whole.

Arrange the selection of fruits on a platter with the bowl of dip in the centre. Serve chilled.

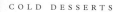
PEARS WITH HONEY AND WINE

California produces several types of honey, the best known being sage blossom and alfalfa. In this Californian recipe, honey sweetens a mulled wine mixture used for stewing pears.

Serves 4

1 bottle of red Zinfandel wine

¾ cup granulated sugar

3 tablespoons clear honey

juice of ½ lemon

1 cinnamon stick

1 vanilla pod, split open lengthwise,
   or a few drops of vanilla extract

2-inch piece pared orange rind

1 whole clove

1 black peppercorn

4 firm ripe pears

whipped cream or sour cream,
   to serve

In a saucepan just large enough to hold the pears standing upright, combine the wine, sugar, honey, lemon juice, cinnamon stick, vanilla pod, orange rind, clove and peppercorn. Heat gently, stirring occasionally, until the sugar has dissolved.

Meanwhile, peel the pears, leaving the core and stem intact on each. Slice a small piece off the base of each pear so that it will stand upright, then gently place the pears in the wine mixture. Simmer the pears uncovered, for 20–35 minutes, depending on size and ripeness. They should be just tender; do not overcook.

With a slotted spoon, gently transfer the pears to a bowl. Continue to boil the poaching liquid until reduced by about half. Let cool, then strain over the pears. Chill for at least 3 hours.

Place the pears in serving dishes and spoon the chilled wine syrup over them. Serve with whipped or sour cream.

COOK'S TIP
Choose pears of similar size and shape for this attractive hot dessert.

Hot Desserts

Friends and family will be buzzing with excitement when you serve these fabulous puddings. Kumquat and honey compote, sweet and creamy rice pudding or fried bananas with honey: every one's a winner!

KUMQUAT AND HONEY COMPOTE

Sun-ripened, warm and spicy ingredients, sweetened with honey, make the perfect winter dessert.

Serves 4

350g/12oz/2 cups kumquats

275g/10oz/1¼ cups dried apricots

30ml/2 tbsp raisins

30ml/2 tbsp lemon juice

1 orange

2.5cm/1in piece of fresh root ginger

4 cardamom pods

4 cloves

30ml/2 tbsp clear honey

15ml/1 tbsp flaked almonds, toasted,
  to decorate

VARIATION

If you prefer, use ready-to-eat dried apricots. Reduce the liquid to 300ml/½pint/1¼cups, and add the apricots for the last 5 minutes of cooking.

Wash the kumquats, and, if they are large, cut them in half. Place them in a large saucepan with the dried apricots and raisins. Pour over 300ml/½ pint/1¼ cups water and add the lemon juice. Bring to the boil.

Pare the rind thinly from the orange and add to the pan. Peel the ginger, grate it finely and add it to the pan. Lightly crush the cardamom pods and add them to the pan, with the cloves.

Lower the heat, cover the pan and simmer gently for about 30 minutes or until the fruit is tender, stirring occasionally.

Squeeze the juice from the orange and add it to the pan with the honey. Stir well, then taste and add more honey if required. Sprinkle with flaked almonds and serve warm.

HONEYED RICE PUDDING

In Spain, Greece, Italy and Morocco rice pudding is a favorite dish, especially when sweetened with honey and flavored with orange.

Serves 4

¼ cup short-grain
   rice

2½ cups milk

2–3 tablespoons clear honey

finely grated rind of ½ small orange

⅔ cup heavy cream

1 tablespoons chopped pistachios,
   toasted, to decorate

Mix the rice with the milk, honey and orange rind in a saucepan. Bring to a boil, then lower the heat, cover and simmer very gently for about 1¼ hours, stirring frequently.

Remove the lid and continue cooking and stirring for 15–20 minutes, until the rice is creamy.

Pour in the cream and simmer for 5–8 more minutes. Serve the rice in individual warmed bowls. Sprinkle each portion with pistachios.

COOK'S TIP
It is important to stir the rice pudding regularly to prevent it from sticking to the bottom of the pan.

FRIED BANANAS WITH HONEY

These delicious treats come from Thailand, where they are sold as snacks throughout the day and night at portable roadside stalls and outdoor markets. Honey acts as a delicious, instant sweet dipping sauce.

Serves 4

1 cup flour

½ teaspoon baking soda

pinch of salt

2 tablespoons sugar

1 egg

2 tablespoons dry shredded coconut
  or 1 tablespoon sesame seeds

4 firm bananas

oil, for frying

mint sprigs and lychees, to decorate

¼ cup clear honey, to serve

VARIATION

Any tender but fairly robust fruit can be given this treatment. Pineapple and apple wedges work well.

Sift the flour, baking soda and salt into a mixing bowl. Stir in the sugar. Whisk in the egg and add enough water (6 tablespoons) to make quite a thin batter. Whisk in the shredded coconut or sesame seeds.

Peel the bananas, then carefully cut each one in half lengthwise, then in half horizontally.

Heat the oil in a wok or deep frying pan. Dip the bananas into the batter, then gently drop a few into the oil. Fry until golden brown. Remove from the oil with a slotted spoon and drain on paper towels. Decorate with mint sprigs and lychees and serve immediately, with the honey for dipping.

SOUFFLEED RICE AND HONEY PUDDING

The fluffy egg whites make an unusually light rice pudding and the delicate honey flavour brings out its creamy deliciousness.

Serves 4

50g/2oz/¼ cup short-grain
   pudding rice
45ml/3 tbsp clear honey
750ml/1¼ pints/3 cups milk
2.5ml/½ tsp vanilla essence
2 egg whites
5ml/1 tsp freshly grated nutmeg

Place the pudding rice, honey and milk in a heavy or non-stick saucepan and bring the milk to the boil. Lower the heat and cover the saucepan. Simmer gently for about 1–1¼ hours, stirring occasionally to prevent the rice sticking, until most of the liquid has been absorbed. Remove the saucepan from the heat.

Stir in the vanilla essence. Preheat the oven to 220°C/425°F/Gas 7.

Place the egg whites in a clean, dry mixing bowl and whisk them until they hold soft peaks. Using a metal spoon or spatula, fold the egg whites evenly into the pudding rice mixture. Pour into a 1 litre/1¾ pint/4 cup ovenproof dish.

Sprinkle the surface of the rice pudding with plenty of freshly grated nutmeg and bake for 15–20 minutes, until it is well-risen and golden brown. Serve hot.

COOK'S TIP

If you've got one, use a vanilla pod instead of the essence. Add it with the honey and remove it before folding in the egg whites.

INDEX

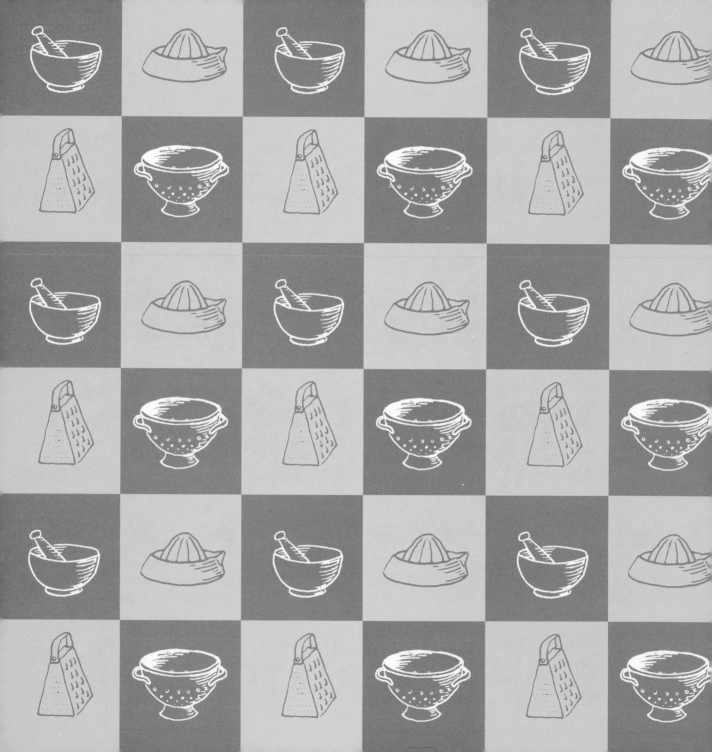